THE FORBIDDEN CITY

Collection of Photographs
by Hu Chui

FOREWORD

As one of the world's ancient civilizations, China has a vast cultural heritage as well as a recorded history that spans five thousand years. Throughout this history, architecture has been one of the key components of China's artistic and cultural traditions, embodying some of the finest and most lasting examples of her achievements in these areas.

The Forbidden City was the royal palace during the last two dynastic periods of China's imperial reign, the Ming and the Qing. The main buildings of the palace were constructed during the Ming dynasty, between the fourth year and the eighteenth year of Emperor Yongle's reign (1406–1420 A.D.). The palace complex is laid out symmetrically along a central axis, and its wooden structures have vermilion walls, yellow–glazed tile roofs and white marble terraces. With more than 9,000 rooms and occupying a total area of 720,000 square meters, it is the largest existing palace complex in the world, and represents a unique Chinese style of architecture.

Twenty–four emperors ruled China from the Forbidden City, which also served as their residence. Everything from the majestic layout of the palace complex to the fine decorative details permeating the structures

was designed to express imperial "supremacy and dignity". Even today, the Forbidden City retains much of its original splendor despite having weathered tremendous changes and turmoil during its nearly six hundred years of existence.

The 1911 Revolution toppled the last monarch, marking the end of imperial rule in China. In 1925, the Palace Museum was established inside the former Forbidden City. This landmark event opened to the general public a place that had been shrouded in mystery for centuries — a place with stately buildings housing countless treasures that were previously enjoyed by a very privileged few. Since then, the Palace Museum has become a monument for all those seeking a glimpse of China's rich past.

February 1995

ABOUT
THE
PHOTOGRAPHER

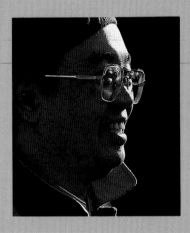

HU CHUI was born in 1952 into a scholarly family in Shanghai, China, and has had a keen interest in photography ever since childhood. In 1969, he was sent to the countryside, where he spent a number of years working as a farmer and manual laborer. During that time, Hu Chui continued with his avid pursuit of photographic art, learning theories and techniques on his own.

In 1978, Hu Chui joined the Palace Museum as a photographer. He later took charge of the Museum's photography studio in 1985. Throughout his career Hu Chui has tirelessly researched and experimented with ways to apply photography — an "imported" and relatively new art form — to the architecture and relics that represent China's ancient civilization. His aim is to break away from the staid approach typically used in the past to photograph such monuments and art objects. In doing so, Hu Chui strives to inspire in the viewer a simultaneous appreciation for the beauty of the objects themselves, and for the artistic medium he uses to capture these images.

Numerous books and award–winning catalogues featuring Hu Chui's photographs of the Palace Museum/Forbidden City have been published and distributed on the Chinese mainland, and in Taiwan, Hong Kong as well as the United States, Japan, Australia and Europe.

Hu Chui is a member of the Chinese Photographers' Association and Secretary General of the Chinese Relic Photography Association.

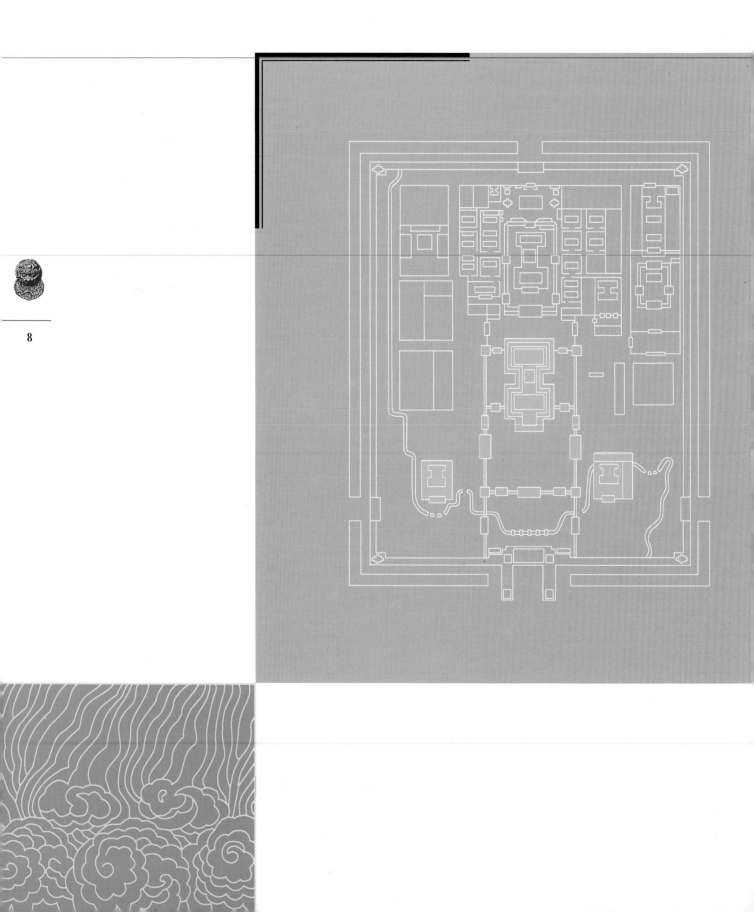

OUTER PALACE

The main structures in the outer palace are the

Hall of Supreme Harmony,

Hall of Complete Harmony and

Hall of Preserving Harmony.

The most outstanding group of palatial

halls in the Forbidden City,

it is where emperors of the Ming and

Qing dynasties handled state affairs

and conducted grand ceremonies.

2

1. *Turret in the Forbidden City / A defensive structure on each of the four corners of the Forbidden City wall, each turret consists of a triple–eaved square tower. The roof of the turret has 72 ridges and 28 eave corners. Unique in design, the turret is a classic of ancient Chinese architecture.*

2. *Mythical figure and animals on a sloping roof ridge / Decorating the eave corners of palatial halls are images of legendary mascots, such as dragon, phoenix, lion, heavenly steed, and sea horse. There is always an odd number — three, five, seven or nine — depending on the rank of the structure. However, to show it holds the highest rank in the Forbidden City, the Hall of Supreme Harmony has ten mascots decorating each of its eave corners.*

14

3. *Hall of Supreme Harmony at dusk /*
The Hall of Supreme Harmony, the
tallest building in the entire palace
complex, symbolizes the suprem-
acy of imperial power.

4. *Gate of Justice (Shunzhenmen) at dawn / The northernmost gate in the Forbidden City, it was used by Inner Palace personnel.*
5. *Snowcapped turret on the northeastern corner of the Forbidden City wall*
6. *Turret on the southeastern corner of the Forbidden City wall*

4

5

6

16

7. *Five–Phoenix Tower at dusk / Meridian Gate, the front gate of the Forbidden City, has five towers, one in the center and two on each side, forming a five–tower structure known as Five–Phoenix Tower. Here the emperor conducted the ceremony for accepting prisoners after winning victory in a major battle.*

8. *Two dragons frolicking with a pearl (detail of a huge stone carving) / The royal passage between flights of stone steps at the front and back of almost all halls in the Forbidden City is carved with dragon, phoenix or cloud designs. The passage could be trod on only by the emperor. The biggest and most exquisitely carved stone passage is at the back of the Hall of Preserving Harmony. It is 17 meters long and weighs 250 tons.*

7

17

8

9. *Square of Supreme Harmony Gate/ The square covers an area of 28,000 square meters. Golden Water River flows across the square, spanned by five white marble bridges. The one in the middle is six meters wide and was used only by the emperor. Civil and military officials could use only the narrower bridges on both sides.*

21

10. View of palace complex / The Forbidden City, the biggest palace complex in the world, occupies an area of
720,000 square meters and has a
total of more than 9,000 rooms.

11. Vermilion palace gate / Each door of
all the palace gates in the Forbidden
City has nine rows of nails, and each
row has nine nails, since nine, as the
biggest single odd number, repre-
sented the dignity of emperors.

12. *The three main halls / The three main halls refer to the Hall of Supreme Harmony, Hall of Complete Harmony and Hall of Preserving Harmony. They all stand on three-tiered terraces of white marble, covering an area of 25,000 square meters. The terraces are in the shape of the Chinese character 土, meaning land. The three halls embody the idea that the emperor is in the center of the land.*

13

15

13. Gate of Supreme Harmony / It is the main entrance to the Outer Palace. In 1644, with the fall of the Ming dynasty, Emperor Shunzhi of the Qing dynasty proclaimed the edict of amnesty at the gate, marking the beginning of the 267–year rule of the Qing dynasty.

14. Bronze lion / One of a pair of bronze lions, 4.36 meters high, that stand in front of the Gate of Supreme Harmony. This pair is the biggest of seven in the Forbidden City.

15. Arch of Golden Water Bridge and its reflection

16

16. *Gate of Supreme Harmony at night*

17. *Bronze crane greeting the morning sun / The crane stands in front of the Hall of Supreme Harmony. Whenever the emperor held court, incense was burned in the belly of the crane and its fragrance escaped through the crane's bill, symbolizing auspiciousness, longevity and an everlasting reign.*

18. *Hall of Supreme Harmony / Here the emperor presided over grand ceremonies and conducted major political activities. When the emperor held court, civil and military officials knelt in front of the hall, with ceremonial guards standing on both sides, creating an atmosphere of imperial dignity.*

17

20

19. Interior view of Hall of Supreme
Harmony / Dragon designs are pro-
fuse in the hall, as ancient Chinese
revered the dragon and emperors
considered them-selves reinc-
arnations of the dragon.

20. Imperial throne in Hall of Supreme
Harmony / The dragon–carved
throne is in the center of the hall.
The emperor sat on the throne when
he held audience with officials.

22

23

33

21. *Hall of Supreme Harmony at night*
22. *Ceiling decoration in Hall of Supreme Harmony*
23. *Caisson in Hall of Supreme Harmony / Decoration on the sunken panels right above the imperial throne.*

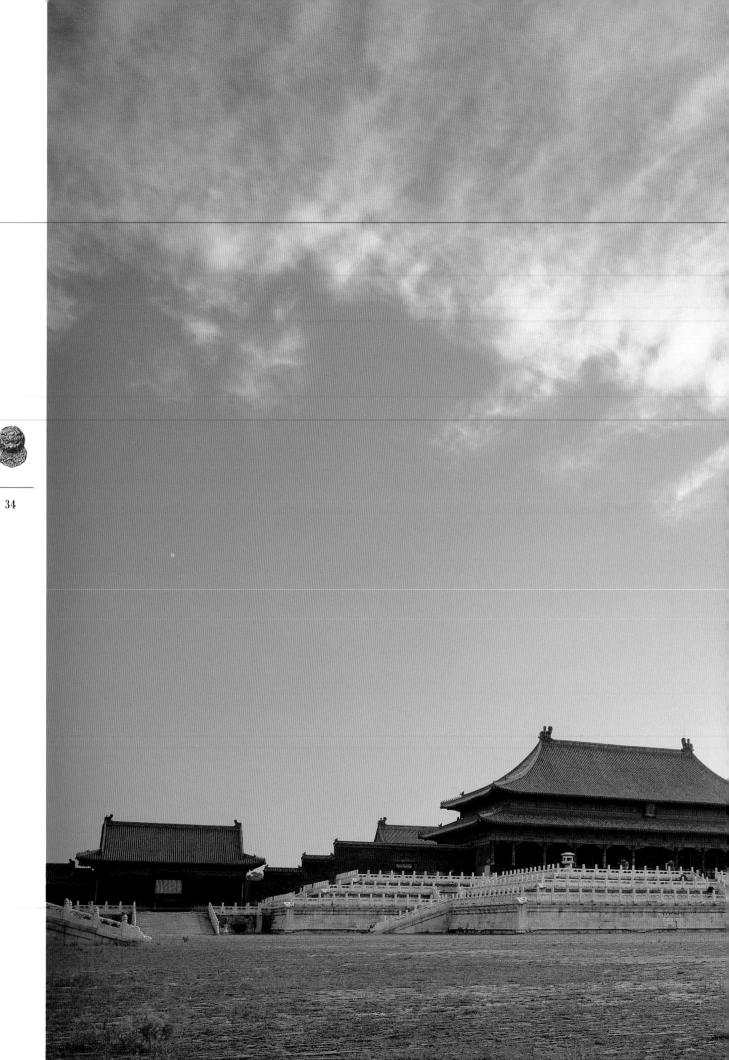

36

24. *Square of Hall of Supreme Harmony*

25

26

25. *Detail of dragon heads on the marble balustrades / This legendary animal was said to be one of the nine sons of the dragon. Here the dragon heads serve as water drains for the three–tiered terraces, giving them both a practical and ornamental function.*
26. *Hall of Complete Harmony and Hall of Preserving Harmony on their marble terraces*

27. Huge stone carving at the back of Hall of Preserving Harmony / The stone carving is 16.6 meters long and 3.07 meters wide, and 1.7 meters thick; it weighs 250 tons. In the early Ming dynasty, when the palace was built, since there were no mechanical tools, it took a little over one month for 10,000 civilian laborers to transport the carving from its work site over 50 kilometers away to the palace building site.

28

29

28. Carved marble balustrades / The three-tiered terraces under the three big halls are 8.13 meters high. Each tier is bordered by a low balustrade. Spaced regularly along the base of the white marble balustrades are waterspouts carved in the shape of dragon heads with a hole in the mouth of each head. During a heavy rain the dragon-head fountains spouting water are a magnificent sight.

29. Gilded water vat in front of right gate of Inner Palace / Big bronze or iron water vats can be seen outside the main halls and palace gates in the Forbidden City. Their function was to store water in case of fire. As most of the vats were exquisitely designed and some gilded, they also served as courtyard furnishings.

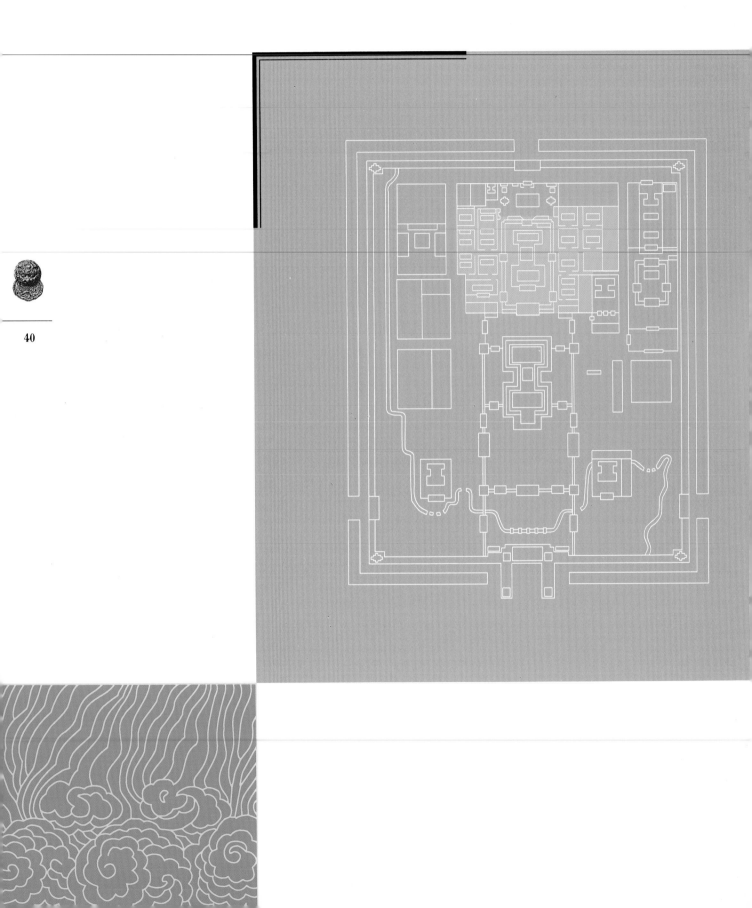

INNER PALACE

The Inner Palace,

the living quarters of emperors and their families,

consists of the Hall of Heavenly Purity, Hall of Union,

Hall of Earthly Peace, and Hall of Mental Cultivation,

flanked by 12 other halls,

six each on the west and east sides.

The buildings in the Inner Palace are not so magnificent

as those in the Outer Palace,

yet they form a compact composition,

creating an atmosphere of mystery and tranquillity.

43

31

32. *Interior view of Hall of Heavenly Purity / Emperors of the Ming and early Qing dynasties used to live in the hall, then it became the site for handling state affairs, receiving greetings and foreign envoys and holding banquets. Since the reign of Emperor Yongzheng of the Qing dynasty the emperor's sealed will designating the heir to the throne was placed behind the plaque saying "Open and Aboveboard" on the rear wall over the throne. The will could not be opened until the death of the emperor, and the name of the new emperor was then made public.*

33

· ·

33. *Hall of Heavenly Purity*
34. *Interior view of Hall of Union / Here the empress received greetings on her birthday, New Year's Day, and Winter Solstice. Displayed in the hall are 25 imperial seals, symbols of imperial power.*

37

36

49

38. *Bridal chamber in Hall of Earthly Peace / The chamber was used by Qing emperors after their wedding ceremonies.*

39. *Screen outside bridal chamber / The red lacquered screen with a golden Chinese character meaning "double happiness" is outside the eastern gate of the Hall of Earthly Peace.*

40

40. *A British–made clock displayed in Hall of Mental Cultivation / Qing emperors were interested in Western articles, including clocks. Many foreign clocks and watches are kept in the Forbidden City.*

41. *Interior view of Hall of Mental Cultivation / From 1723, the first year of the Yongzheng reign of the Qing dynasty, until 1911, the third year of Emperor Xuantong's reign, the hall served as both the emperor's bedchamber and the site to handle state affairs. In 1911 Empress Longyu declared the abdication of the emperor, thus ending the 267–year rule of the Qing dynasty.*

43. East Chamber of Warmth in Hall of
Mental Cultivation / When Qing emperor Xianfeng died and was succeeded by five-year-old Zai Chun,
known as Emperor Tongzhi, Empress
Dowager Cixi staged a palace coup
and took the reins of government.
The East Chamber of Warmth was

42

54

43

42. Gate of Mental Cultivation / The
front gate of the Hall of Mental
Cultivation. No one was allowed to
enter it unless summoned by the
emperor.

where Cixi "conducted state affairs from behind a curtain". The practice was for the child emperor to sit symbolically on his throne in front, while Cixi and another empress dowager, Ci'an, sat behind a curtain, listening to reports of court ministers and giving instructions. Though the two dowagers seemed on a par, real power was in the hands of Cixi. After three–year–old Zai Tian succeeded Zai Chun as Emperor Guangxu, Cixi continued to rule "behind a curtain."

44. *Rear chamber of Hall of Mental Cultivation / The Hall of Mental Cultivation is shaped like the Chinese character 工. Beginning with Emperor Yongzheng, successive emperors of the Qing dynasty used the hall's rear chamber as their bedchamber.*

45. *Emperor's bedchamber in Hall of Mental Cultivation*

46. *Studio of Three Rarities in Hall of Mental Cultivation / This room used to be the emperor's study. Later it was called Studio of Three Rarities because Qing emperor Qianlong stored there copybooks with the work of Wang Xizhi, Wang Xianzhi and* Wang Xun, three great calligraphers in Chinese history. In the room hangs a plaque with the studio's name in the handwriting of Emperor Qianlong.

47. *Furnishings of Hall of Mental Cultivation*

45

57

46

47

49. *Bronze dragon in front of Hall of Preserved Elegance / This bronze dragon was cast in 1884, the tenth year of the reign of Qing emperor Guang-xu, to celebrate the fiftieth birthday of Empress Dowager Cixi. The dowager moved from the Hall of Eternal Spring to the Hall of Preserved Elegance in October that year.*

49

50

61

51

52

62

50. *Hall of Preserved Elegance / One of the six western halls in the Inner Palace. Cixi lived in this hall when she first entered the palace. In the hall's rear chamber she gave birth to Zai Chun, who later became Emperor Tongzhi. As the emperor's mother, Cixi rose quickly to a prominent position. she was popularly known as the Western Dowager, because she lived for years in the western halls.*

51. *Interior view of Hall of Preserved Elegance / The Hall of Preserved Elegance was the most luxuriously furnished and decorated building in the Forbidden City. When Empress Dowager Cixi lived there, she was waited on by more than 50 eunuchs, palace maids and servants day and night.*

52. *Interior view of Hall of Ultimate Origin (Taijidian) / One of the six western halls containing bedchambers of the empress and royal concubines. Cixi once lived there.*
53. *Furnishings of Hall of Ultimate Origin*

56

54. *Furnishings of Hall of Eternal Spring*

55. *Interior view of Hall of Eternal Spring / The empress or royal concubines lived here. It served as the residence of Empress Dowager Cixi during the reigns of emperors Tongzhi and Guangxu.*

56. *Hall of Health and Harmony (Yihexuan) / Built in 1772, the 37th year of the reign of Qing emperor Qianlong, this hall was in the architectural complex designed as Emperor Qianlong's residence after retirement.*

57. *Chamber of Enchanting Scenery (Li-jingxuan) on a rainy night / Emperor Tongzhi was born in this chamber. Later his mother, Cixi, became a powerful empress dowager and ruled China for over 40 years.*

57

58

59

. . . .

58. *Gate of Quintessence (Zhongcuimen)*
59. *Hall of Quintessence (Zhongcui-
    gong) / This hall served as the crown
    prince's residence when it was first
    built early in the Ming dynasty. In
    the Qing dynasty it became one of the
    six eastern halls, serving as living
    quarters for the empress and royal
    concubines. Empress Dowager Ci'an
    was known as the Eastern Dowager,
    because she lived in this hall from the
    time she entered the palace.*

60

60. *Gate of Auspicious Beginning (Qixiangmen)*

61. *Furnishings of Hall of Preserved Elegance / The Hall of Preserved Elegance, residence of Empress Dowager Cixi, was renovated and refurnished on a large scale during the reigns of emperors Tongzhi and Guangxu. The dowager held the celebration for her fiftieth birthday in this hall.*

62. *Furnishings of Hall of Fragrance (Shufangzhai) / This hall, tastefully furnished with a wooden openwork partition, was where the emperor and empress watched opera performances and had their meals.*

61

63. *Multitreasure cabinet in Hall of Fragrance / The cabinet, reaching to the ceiling, contains small compartments in various geometric shapes. It was used in the Forbidden City as both an embellishment and a shelf for displaying valuable objects.*

64. *Hall of Norms of Government (Huangjidian) / Built in the 41st year of the reign of Qing emperor Qianlong, this hall is the main structure in the architectural complex designed as Emperor Qianlong's residence after his retirement. Emperor Qianlong held the famous "banquet for a thousand elders" in this hall.*

65. *Gate of Peace and Longevity (Ningshoumen) / Modeled on the Gate of Heavenly Purity, the main gate to the Inner Palace, the Gate of Peace and Longevity leads to the Hall of Norms of Government and northward to the architectural complex designed as Emperor Qianlong's retirement residence. Outside the gate is a courtyard planted with pines and cypresses, symbolizing longevity.*

66. Nine-Dragon Wall viewed from outside Gate of Norms of Government / Ancient Chinese worshiped the dragon as a totem, and Chinese emperors claimed to be dragon incarnate. In the Forbidden City dragon sculptures and designs are everywhere. Nine-Dragon Wall has the largest group of glazed dragon sculptures in high relief.

66

73

65

67. Bird's–eye view of Imperial Garden / The Imperial Garden was a private garden on the central axis of the Forbidden City. During the Ming and Qing dynasties dependants of the imperial family were not free to go out of the palace, so the Imperial Garden was their favorite place for taking a stroll.

67

68. Bird's-eye view of Imperial Garden / The Imperial Garden was a private garden on the central axis of the Forbidden City. During the Ming and Qing dynasties dependants of the imperial family were not free to go out of the palace, so the imperial Garden was their favorite place for taking a stroll.

69. Ceiling of theater of Hall of Fragrance

70. *Theater of Hall of Fragrance / This theater was built in the first year of the reign of Qing emperor Qianlong in the courtyard of the Hall of Fragrance in the northwestern corner of the Imperial Garden. The emperor, empress dowager and imperial family dependants often went there to watch opera performances.*

71. *Theater of Pavilion of Melodious Voice (Changyinge) / This is the largest theater in the Forbidden City, with three stories (named Prosperity, High Position, and Longevity) aboveground and five deep wells underground to enhance sound effects. Opera performances were held here on festive and other occasions each year.*

72. *Theater of Hall of Retirement (Juanqinzhai)*

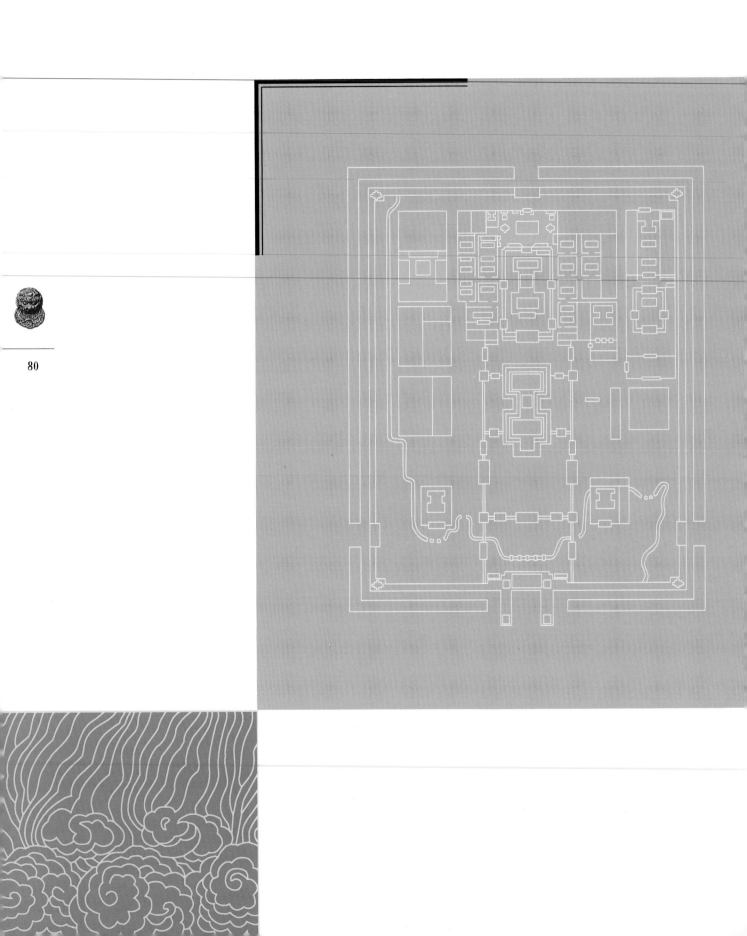

PALACE GARDENS

The gardens in the Forbidden City,

connected by halls and courtyards,

are an important component of the palace complex.

Each different, the gardens, shaded by aged trees,

contained pavilions, towers, corridors

and rockeries and were ideal places

for the emperor and his dependants to relax

and enjoy themselves.

73

74

76

75. *Imperial Pavilion for Viewing the Scenery (Yujingting) / Built on the top of a manmade hill in the northeastern corner of the Imperial Garden, this pavilion provides a place for looking far into the distance. Dependants of the imperial family, confined to the Forbidden City all year round, would go up to the pavilion and enjoy a distant view to relieve homesickness on the Double Ninth Festival, a day for ascending heights, each year.*

76. *Pavilion of Everlasting Spring (Wanchunting)*

77. *Garden of Hall for Consolation of Mothers (Cininghuayuan) / This garden was built in an area where the empresses and concubines of deceased emperors lived. It contained mostly halls for worshiping Buddha.*

78. *Pavilion of Paramount Elegance (Songxiuting) This pavilion was built on a manmade hill in the third courtyard of Emperor Qianlong's garden, a private garden in the architectural complex in the northeastern part of the Forbidden City where Qianlong lived after his retirement.*

79

80

79. *View of Emperor Qianlong's garden*
80. *Pavilion for Bestowing Wine (Xishangting) / Built in the first court-yard of Emperor Qianlong's garden, this pavilion has a* baosha *(Chinese-style portico) in front and a stream inside. On Xiuxi Day (third day of the third lunar month) the emperor and his scholar friends would come here and sit by the stream, on which a cup of wine drifted. When the cup stopped in front of someone, he would pick it up, drink the wine and improvise a poem. This practice was initiated in the days of Wang Xizhi, a great calligrapher of the Eastern Jin dynasty.*
81. *Ginkgo tree in garden of Hall for Consolation of Mothers.*

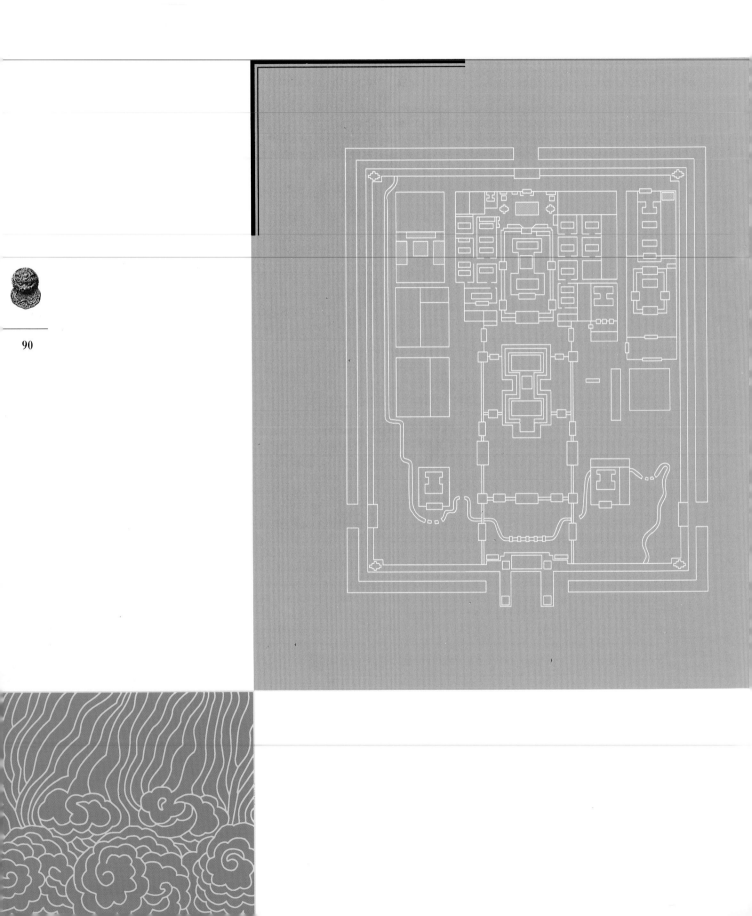

HALLS OF WORSHIP

Though Lamaism (Tibetan Buddhism)

was established

as the state religion early in the Qing dynasty,

Buddhist and Taoist images,

as well as the image of Tsongkapa,

were enshrined and worshiped

in the Forbidden City.

82

. . . .

82. *Interior view of Hall of Imperial Peace (Qin'andian) / Enshrined in this hall was the image of Supreme Master Zhengwu, the Taoist God of Water. Every year at the beginning of spring, summer, autumn and winter, or the lst, 7th, 13th and 19th solar terms, the emperor would come here to burn incense and pray to the god for fire protection.*

83

84

83. Hall of Imperial Peace / First built in the Ming dynasty, this hall has a history of over 570 years. On the railings and balusters around the hall's foundation are exquisite carvings of the Ming dynasty.

84. Hall of Omnipresent Luck (Xianruoguan), a place for worshiping Buddha

85. Enamel dagoba in Pavilion of Flowers of Western Heavens (Fanhualou) / The Pavilion of Flowers of Western Heavens was one of the buildings for worshiping Lamaist Buddhism in the Forbidden City. Built in 1772, the 37th year of the reign of Qing emperor Qianlong, it is a two–story pavilion, the lower story containing six enamel dagobas exquisitely made by craftsmen in the Qing palace.

86. Moat of Forbidden City / The Forbidden City is surrounded by a 52–meter–wide moat, which served as the first line of defense.

85

图书在版编目(CIP)数据

故宫：胡锤摄影作品集：英文／胡锤摄，－北京：中国摄影出版社，
1998.4 重印
ISBN 7-80007-153-7

Ⅰ.故… Ⅱ.胡… Ⅲ.故宫－摄影集－英文 Ⅳ.J426.1
中国版本图书馆 CIP 数据核字(98)第 03893 号

THE FORBIDDEN CITY
Collection of Photographs by Hu Chui

Managing editor:	Ren Yiquan
Designer:	Wan Yatsha
	Beijing Shuttle Graphic Designing Technology Co. Ltd.
Translators:	Yang Aiwen, Wang Xingzheng
Publishers:	China Photographic Publishing House
Printed by:	C & C Offset Printing Co. (Shenzhen) Ltd.
Specially appointed general distributor:	Acoustic Guide Gugong Ltd.